ISBN: 978-1-909833-33-3

www.themulberrycollection.co.uk

# Dedication

This book is dedicated to
Karen, Alastair, Charles, Duncan
The children of
Malcolm Campbell Irvine
1943 - 1996
'I flourish in Light and in Shade'

# THE MULBERRY COLLECTION 'ROMNEY MARSH LYRICS'

## CONTENTS

## Autumn:

## Winter:

# RETURN TO THE ROMNEY MARSH

I often long to return to the marsh
With its sway of wild iris and tall bristling grasses

To the smell of the earth…herons in flight
There is great beauty here, which nothing surpasses

Silently threading through patchwork fields
Are winding lanes, with green velvet edges

In evening light, sheep close-crop fine meadows
And nearby, small creatures nestle in hedges

Wildflowers jostle in rhythmic time…
Long evening shadows give way to soft night

All sounds then lull…the moon dances alone
'Till songbirds declare, the first morning light

# ONSET OF SPRING

Nestling beneath hedgerows

Snowdrops announce the onset of spring

The daffodils' floral trumpets dance gold across meadows

As soft greens unfurl…

Wild iris rustle and sway with dyke reeds

And in dappled shade, bluebells stand silent and serene…

A gentle wind stirs the boughs and blossoms spiral like snow

Pastel, perfumed, swirling flurries of delight, dance on the breeze

Clouds of hawthorn and cow parsley hover above the dykes

And later, buttercups will drench nearby fields

# SPRING

Greens unfurl, as Earth wakes from winter sleep

A warm breeze stirs

And a gentle sun greets each new leaf

They glisten like multi-facet emeralds

As they adorn the waking boughs

Country lanes are dressed snow-white

By blackthorn winter hedgerows

Rape spreads her mantle

And marsh fields glow with rippling gold

Startled rabbits freeze

Then dart in hedgerows

Partridge scuttle to hide in fields

Regal swans proudly build their nest

And young lambs bleat

Their cries are carried through the haze, softly

On the gentle, gathering breeze

# DAWN CHORUS

You can tell when it's the morning
That's when the orchestra begins

The chirruping and calling
And the beat of tiny wings

Softly at first, the birds strike up their morning tune
Music whilst still quite dark, will chase away the moon

The symphony grows louder by the dawning of the day
Wild birdsong fills the air, as they all begin to play

No one sees a 'baton' or the 'leader' at all
Pitch and tone is perfect, there's never any flaw

Each member of the orchestra excels at his own part
Every artist plays his score, from the centre of his heart

And the beauty of the songs
from our friends upon the wing

Fills our hearts with joy
so our hearts begin to sing!

# MARSHLAND SPRINGTIME

Sweet smelling 'May' blossom and slender cow parsley
Together line marshland fields
Golden reeds stand tall and proud
Rape blossom stretches for miles, promising a bumper yield

Blackthorn blossom now spent
Is overtaken by bright spring leaves
New wheat stands strong and green
Where last autumn, farmers cast their seed

Blackberry boughs are waking…
Joining the happy throng
Marshland birds soar and dip
Delighting us with each new song

Telegraph poles with wires that sing
Stand eerily in morning mist
Hedgerows alive with busy birds
Are waiting for the sun's warm kiss

Moorhens scuttle across water
Leaving ripples in their wake
Hoping that I, a stranger, miss
Where they've chosen their nest to make…

Spider webs, shine like crystal jewels
In the misty morning light
Overhead, the geese return
Chattering loudly, whilst in flight

The morning marshland silence
Is broken too, by the distant rolling waves
Which joins the bleating of lambs and birdsong
To declare the new spring day

# THE DAWN OF SPRING

The black ink of night
Melts into soft grey
Marooned at a country station
I watch the birth of a new day

All is still and quiet
The damp air is cold
The only sound the waking birds
Their calls are bright and bold

The gabled, red-bricked building
Is quietly sleeping still
Alone, I watch the sunrise
Through the haze beyond the hill

At this time of contemplation
Mist around me curls
I marvel at the glorious sight
Which before my eyes unfurls

The pale grey sky far in the east
The sun is changing as I gaze…
Her silent brush strokes tint the clouds
With colours that amaze

Treasuring these precious moments
Before the onset of the day
I feel privileged to witness
Nature whilst at play

# FIRST LIGHT

In the soft lilac of a frozen dawn

I crunch my way across glistening, pink shingle

Gazing east, I watch silently

As the orange crescent of the rising sun

Pierces the horizon,

Heralding all the promise of a new day

The quiet waters break

White fringed, along the foreshore

The continual murmur of the tide is broken too

By the lone cry of a gull,

Who dips and soars above land and sea

To show, he is Master of the morning

Too soon, the colour of the sunrise fades

And the moment of magic is past

13

# COLOURDANCE

It's time for the Ox-eye daises to swirl across the land

Hand in hand with buttercups, dancing to the country band

With a flash of scarlet ribbon, poppies join in the rhythmic dance

Slender, tall, cow-parsley sways in time…waiting to take a chance

May blossom rises up, to join the happy throng

If you listen carefully, you'll hear their joyful song

Gently the warmth of the rising sun, wakes others from winter slumbers

Our eyes rejoice as colours abound, in ever increasing numbers

All the dancing is strictly in time, with the heartbeat of

Mother Earth

Take my hand and come with me

Let's celebrate…and dance for all our worth!

# MORNING LIGHT

Clouds, soft grey, roll gently seaward

Allowing the sun's rays

To momentarily pierce the horizon

Reflections instantly ripple across wet sand

As light brings life and colour to all

The shingle echoes deep

Crunching beneath solitary feet

Gulls rest on shining sand

And breakwaters cast long shadows

Reaching out like outstretched fingers

Trying to grasp and hold

The morning light

# AT THE END OF THE DAY

Late afternoon sun, paints sand gold
Hungry seagulls, are growing bold

Footprints are scattered, in wet sand
Some castles are small, others, grand

Seashells glint, in evening light
Some quite dull but others, bright

Seagulls like stars, edge the shore
Although they're fed, they beg for more!

White-fringed surf endlessly turns
Now, the sun no longer burns

Gathered treasures, abandoned by all
Still the seagulls loudly call

The warm wind, drops and cools
Lost toys lie, in salty pools

A lone-kite, distant, flying high
The setting sun, tints the sky

Aqua, pink and purple clouds
The beach is mine...gone are the crowds

# EVENING LIGHT

Shafts of golden, evening sun light up the emerald fields

Kissing the wheat and barley, blessing their future yields

Majestic, purple clouds roll and fill the aqua sky

Elderflowers nod, to acknowledge pheasants passing by

In nearby dykes, reflections of yellow iris sway

And safe, on an island of reeds, swans and cygnets play

The wind gathers momentum, reeds and grasses no longer still

Far off, a cuckoo softly calls, from his home beyond the hill

As I watch the scene, the sun then slips behind a cloud

So I turn to face the west and whisper my thanks aloud

# PRECIOUS MOMENTS

The seagulls, they are sleeping now

And the salty air has cooled

The aqua sky now faded,

No longer shines like crystal jewels

There's great beauty in the stillness

At this special time of day

And I revel in the silence

Now, that all have ceased to play

They are such precious moments these

At the closing of the day

For then, I listen with my heart

To all God has to say...

# EARLY MORNING FREEDOM

One may cross the road with ease, to smell flowers, without fear
Pigeons remain on the fence even though you draw near

Small birds may flutter but they don't fly away
You'll hear their chorus as they welcome the day

Pause at the dyke, reeds will sing you a song
Nearby, ducks gather in their own happy throng

Seagulls tussle in the brightening sky
Small reed birds chatter, away from your eyes

A motionless willow holds court on the green
And beside it a sycamore, silent, serene…

As you walk winding pathways, grasses whisper 'hello'
Ahead, startled rabbits dive in burrows below

Golden grasses abound, yet, apart from the crowd
The bright yellow ragwort, stands tall and proud

And then you reach it…the coast, with its waves
As the sun tints all gold, in its beauty you'll bathe

The smell of the ocean will greet you mid-air
And this glorious marsh beauty is all ours, to share!

# AUTUMN MIGRATION

Early morning sunrise, burns off autumnal mist

Colour starts to live once more, where the sun has kissed

A flock of starlings lightly balances on the wire

Their leader lectures them to raise their courage higher

With their birds-eye view of marshland fields and sand

They all prepare to travel, to far-off, distant lands

Their hearts full of courage, I watch those small birds rise

Seconds later, a cloud of starlings fills the sky

As they sweep and roll, aloft, more birds then join in

Soaring in unison, as their journeys they begin

# AUTUMN ON THE ROMNEY MARSH

Clouds…sugar pink and lavender
Against an aqua sky.

Each…one of nature's delights
Shared with you and I.

Stark…against the skyline
A lone, wind-ravaged tree.

Breath…snatched greedily, deeply,
From air that's wild and free.

Grasses…a russet-coloured carpet
Stretches mile upon mile.

Sheep…stand like silent boulders
With faces that beguile.

Crumbling…red brick field barns
Proclaim another age.

Autumn…dressed in vibrant colours,
Numbers impossible to gauge.

Curving…dykes and hedges
Of interminable length.

England's…pleasant land
Speaks with quiet, sacred strength.

# AUTUMN'S SILENCE

Dark blackberries glisten
Hanging heavily on briars
Nearby, hawthorn berries glow
As if, they're now on fire

Hazelnuts are falling
Softly to the ground
Mushrooms, scattered everywhere
Are pure ~ and white ~ and round

Seed heads dance, gently in the breeze
Rivers tumble on and on...towards the sea
It's early morning ~ quiet ~ calm
This, to my soul, a healing balm

Apples are ripening upon the trees
Starlings swoop and glide with ease

The village green is empty
Lofty pigeons call
Roses 'round the cottage doors
Flow, like waterfalls

Silence is the keeper
Silence is the key
Listen to the silence
It speaks to you ~ and me

# PREPARING FOR HARVEST

Wheel-tracks curve through rippling fields
Earth's almost ready to surrender her yield

In the pink new light of the approaching dawn
Poppies unite in fields of bright corn

Elderflower blossom gives way to new fruit
Small sheep replace lambs once so cute

A cloud of birds swiftly rises in flight
They prepare for a journey, which exhausts their might

The breath of the Dog Rose no more plays in the air
Young calves, still perplexed, continue to stare

Reeds have been cut, dykes are now cleared
Gone is the hide from which bullfrogs once peered

Blackberries to pick and sloes to distil
Soon trucks will pass by on their way to the mill

Bristling grasses, wide open skies
We relish this beauty before our eyes

# EARTH'S CLEANSING

The dykes are full and the tide is high
Black clouds fill the rolling sky

Telephone poles teeter on pointed toes
The wind whips up a sea of foam

Eerily shrieking her mighty wrath
She spirals upwards the salty froth

Hedgerows lean and block the road
Broken gates defy the country code

White rain blinds and obscures the view
Crouching churches defend silent pews

Sheep are moved to higher ground
Farmers battle with morning rounds

Fields are flooded, signs are askew
Nature struggles to cleanse the Earth anew

She begs her message be understood
For pollution fills her skies and destroys her woods

Into her open wounds we pour in haste
Our tons of man-made fetid waste

How long I wonder, can we afford
To allow nature's plight to be ignored?

# HARVEST CALL

Golden sun pierces deep shade
In twisting tunnels of softly arched trees
Ragwort nods rhythmically
In time, with the late summer breeze

In a far-off field...
Dust clouds swirl high into warm air
As mammoth farm machinery
Strip once-nurtured fields, now bare

Lone trees mark the horizon
Stark, in regimental stance
Marsh reeds and telephone wires
In gathering wind do dance

Farmers hasten to harvest crops
Before the onset of autumn rain
Multi-racial flocks of birds
Happily feast on wayward grain

Cow Parsley rebelliously
Expels its precious seed
And the land gives way to autumn
To fulfil our basic needs

# MILLENNIUM NIGHT 2000

In a windless coastal curve we stood
On the beach at Romney Bay
With giant candles in our hands
Waiting to herald a special day
Close to midnight was the hour
Mist around us swirled
Helium balloons flew high aloft
Their ribbons 'round us curled
The champagne cork was gently eased
Glasses poised in easy reach
Mysterious silence deepened now
To those scattered on the beach
Breathing in the stillness
Soft silence waiting The Millennium Hour
Distant lights traced the horizon
From Dover Cliffs to Dungeness Power
Then, suddenly, it was over
The year of ninety-nine
2000 then leapt forward
And all began to shine
The champagne cork flew in the sky
Balloons begged their release
We filled our glasses, raised them high
In our circle of light on the beach
Fireworks leapt and swirled and showered
Collective wishes running wild
A coloured myriad of joy
Was shared by you and I
And at that precious moment
Love burst and raced across the sky
And the most amazing thing that night?
United in thought – The whole world smiled

# A MYSTICAL, MAGICAL, MARSHLAND NIGHT

Unable to sleep
I rose
Stepping out, into the magical night
And there floated I
Poised on deck
Like a bird in mystical flight
My breath froze
I slowly raised my disbelieving eyes
A myriad of stars shone
In the silent, velvet sky
I stood there
In frozen silence
Staring in great delight
Stars would fade...
Then, reappear
Weaving magic in the night
Frost rose
Then, stole towards me
Anxious to claim another prize
I pulled my robe still closer
But could not tear away my eyes
This mystical, magical, marshland night
Was to me a gift
Kindly given
My heart spoke its thanks
To those whom
I love...
Residing in God's glorious heaven

# MARSHLAND STORM

Mystical, magical, swirling rain
Beats noisily against the window pane

I hear it…as it gurgles and splutters
Magnified sounds, in pipes and gutters

The wind buffets and bangs, lifts and sweeps
Teasing the torrents ~ as I try to sleep!

Distant clouds roll and thunder
Lightening dances, as I gaze in wonder…

Safe in bed, in the warm, I'll wait
Until the storm is done

Later, fresh from sleep I will wake
To be greeted ~ by the rising sun

# FROZEN SILENCE

The frozen moon is haloed

In a white and misty sky

And ghostly trees are huddled

In their family groups, nearby

A pair of darting foxes

Appear now in the glow

To follow rabbit footprints

Clearly marked out in the snow

The mist is like a cloak of silence

Settled all around

And in that frozen silence

My beating heart's the only sound

# SNOWSCENE

Snowflakes dance in patterns
And float...to frozen ground

A blanket of crystal white
Settles, for miles around

Gentle, muffled footfalls
Can softly, now be heard

The snowflakes swirling in the sky
Are like a giant cauldron...stirred

Ivy rustles in the icy wind
Offering a glimpse of emerald green

Woodland creatures are hiding now...
Though their tracks are clearly seen

The snow settles deftly, on branches high
Forming a myriad of crystal domes

The curl and scent of fruit-wood smoke
Shall guide us safely home

# WINTER SUNSET

Late one winter Sunday afternoon
A heartfelt message makes me raise my eyes
Clouds the colours of summer fruits
I see ripple across the sky

Sweet smoke from fruitwood curls aloft
And jet trails, one moment so defined
The next, dissolve like watercolours
Illustrating the fragility of mankind

Mulberry, oak and ash stand sharp and black
Silhouetted in the last throes of the day
Their hands raised forever upward
All determined to have their say

The cold air is clean, silent and still
After a lavish farewell, the sun fades in size
And as I watch my heart hears distant echoes
As in other lands, they watch her beauty rise

# A WINTER WALK

I went for a walk in the woods today
The trees were all covered in white
It was cold and on the ground lay deep snow
It was such a glorious sight

It was silent in the forest
No animals or birds could I hear
But I clearly sensed their presence
As from deep-secret burrows they'd peer

I was watched by many pairs of eyes
Of rabbits, field mice and shrew
The further into the woods I walked
The deeper the silence grew...

Eerie in that wonderland
Trees were clad in their finest of gowns
All dressed up and looking so grand
Whilst weakly, the sun lit the ground

As I raised my eyes up high
I saw their bowers all covered in snow
They formed a temple in the sky for me...
Then watched my Spirit grow

# Other books in this series by Patricia Irvine available from www.themulberrycollection.co.uk

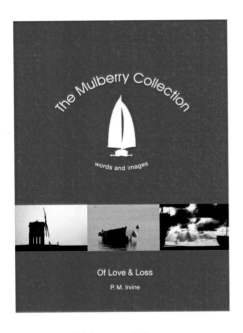

Of Love & Loss

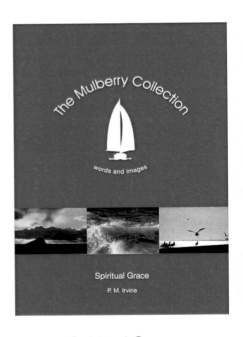

Spiritual Grace